CW01643423

O[illegible]

THE LIGHTNING TREE

Chris Howkins

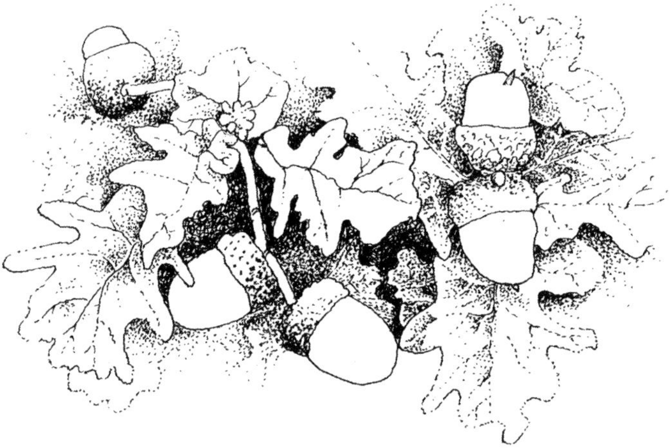

Published by
Chris Howkins

COPYRIGHT
Text and illustrations © Chris Howkins 2006

PUBLISHER
Chris Howkins, 70 Grange Road, New Haw, Addlestone, Surrey, KT15 3RH

PRINTER
Hobbs the Printers Ltd., Brunel Road, Southampton, Hampshire,
SO40 3WX

CONDITIONS OF SALE
This book is sold subject to the condition that it shall not, by way of trade or otherwise, be lent, re-sold, hired out or otherwise circulated in any form of binding or cover other than that in which it is published and without a similar condition including this condition being imposed upon the subsequent purchaser.

ALL RIGHTS RESERVED
No part of this publication may be reproduced, stored in a retrieval system, or transmitted in any form or by any means electronic, mechanical, photocopying, recording or otherwise without the prior permission of the publisher.

ISBN-10 1 901087 70 0
ISBN-13 978 1 901087 70 3

CONTENTS

INTRODUCTION

Why is it that of all the trees in the British Isles it is the oak that we hold dearest? Nowadays, if somebody proposes cutting down a tree there are likely to be objections. If it is an oak tree there will be protests. If it is one of those *leylandii* conifers then people will come and help! As a nation we do not cherish conifers but we will fight for an oak. Why? What is so special about oak trees?

The answer to that is not modern. The material in the 'history' section of my database is in chronological order and the eye can run back and back seeing a continuum of appreciation of this tree – through the great age of ship-building and England's famous 'wooden walls', to Elizabeth I passing conservation laws in favour of the oak, to the great medieval builders seeking mighty oaks for building cathedrals, to early Christian missionaries vying with the heathens over 'superstitious' veneration of oak trees sacred to them, to the days of 'tree worship' by the Saxons, and Vikings and so into the Iron Age and the beliefs of the Irish Celts, and the Bronze Age with the stunning find of the oaken 'Seahenge'.[1] From the preceding Stone Age we get a realisation that the people knew an oak tree from any other. That comes from the discovery in 1991 of a Stone Age man preserved in the ice high in the Alps. He lived about 5,300 years ago and has become known as the Iceman.[2] He interests me because he was dressed and carried with him, clothing and artefacts made from plants. From our knowledge of those plants today we admire his choice but there is more to it than that, for it shows us that Stone Age people were discerning. They learned to distinguish one species of plant from another and the nature of the plant's characteristics and how to exploit them. Thereby it gives us an insight into childhood education all those thousands of years ago, when children growing up had this knowledge passed on to them by their elders. We also know, from little Stone Age humanoid sculptures, dubbed 'Venuses', that they believed in supernatural forces, gods if you like. Through all this runs the thread of our quest.

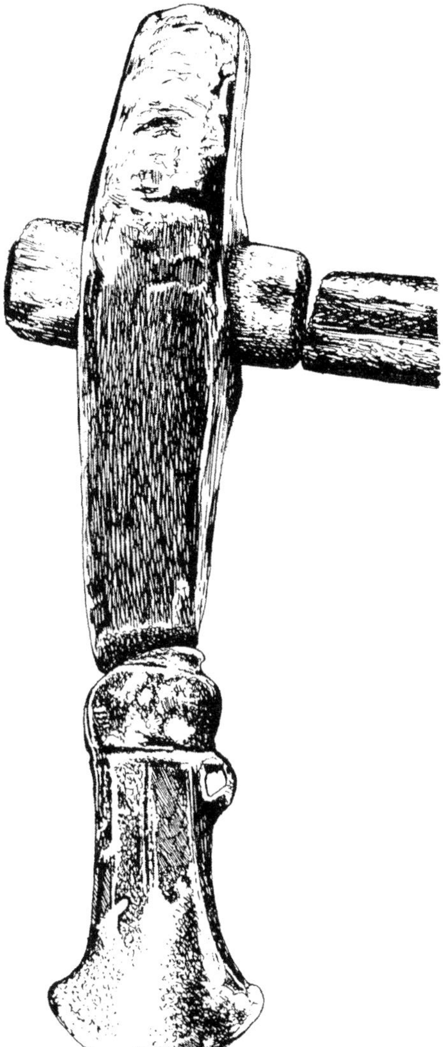

This amazing axe came with some other finds out of the Thames gravels between Chertsey and Shepperton. It is a Bronze Age axe that had most of its woodwork intact – very rare indeed. There was more handle than shown here.

The bronze axe head is fixed to a wooden head-piece which is made of oak. That is just as we would expect since oak is so strong at taking impact on its end-grain. The handle is made of ash which again is the best choice because it absorbs inpact vibrations. This tool was made to be effective, made to last, and made to be comfortable to use.

These qualities had the laboratory scientists very excited by the time I went to collect the axe from conservation treatment in East London, on behalf of Chertsey Museum. It is now part of the Museum collections.

THE LIGHTNING TREE

When I was little my mother used to say that thunder was the noise of God shifting his furniture around. That was perfectly understandable to anybody who had experienced my mother cleaning, as a reaction to being annoyed. Furniture rumbled! It's a very ancient idea. Very early people were unnerved by thunderstorms with their lightning strikes that set fire to the landscape. The lightning was a link between earth and the great forces they believed were above. Lightning came to be seen as a message from the gods. It was also observed that lightning struck oak trees more often than any other species and so oak trees became sacred to the great sky gods in the differing cultures stretching right across Europe and into Asia.

Today there are those who question whether lightning really does strike oak trees most often but surveys of blasted trees to quantify one species against another have shown that there are more blasted oaks than any other species. There is a 'but' to this argument though. Oaks are famously durable and so the evidence survives for longer than for other species. Furthermore, oaks are difficult to set alight – visit a hollow oak and the chances are high that the inside bears evidence of charring from an attempt to fire it. The fire went out and the tree lived on, holding its evidence. An ash and a willow struck by lightning when I was a child both went up in flames to their near complete destruction in a spectacular and unforgettable way. That said, the cultural evidence from earliest times associates oaks with lightning, across the cultures. They can't all be wrong surely? Certainly the tree venerated in terms of the sky gods, and in particular the thunder and lightning gods, was the oak.

CELTS AND DRUIDS

From where I am writing, in northern Surrey, I am between the Iron Age hillforts on St. George's Hill at Weybridge and on St. Anne's Hill at Chertsey.[3] The people who built them and used them seem very remote but the end of the Iron Age is that period described as 'Celtic' and that emotive word brings many a reader's mind to life. Archaeologists would like to strangle it. The term suggests unity, a common culture, a specific people, which is indeed what was first thought. Archaeology has moved on, to the point where diversity in the evidence means the term is best cremated. Nevertheless, whether we call them Late Iron Age or Celtic they were definitely there. These were the British people who drove off the first Roman invasion of 54 BCE and accommodated the second in 43 CE.[4]

The term 'Roman Britain' is another absurdity, since it implies that the invasion wiped out the British whereas the two cultures learned to live side by side – the Romano-British period. The Romans were initially a military force, not a plough-team; they *needed* the British to carry on farming to produce the food. They were very good at it. The productivity of the land must have given them great faith in their fertility rituals and if we look among their deities for a great sky god who was associated with lightning and oak trees we do indeed find one. Julius Caesar writing about Gaul, recorded him:

'of all the gods they most worship Mercury. He has the largest number of images, and they regard him as the inventor of all the arts, as their guide on the roads and in travel, and as chiefly influential in making money and in trade'. [5]

Even without giving us the native name it has been possible, using other sources, to conclude that Caesar's Gaulish 'Mercury' was Lug/Lugu/Lugus/Lugh/Lleu/Llewellys. He is still commemorated in hundreds of place names right across Europe, from Ireland and Wales to Legnica in Poland. The name variations change according to geographical location but are believed to refer to the same deity. That makes it the only deity of the time that transcended the European cultures which otherwise had their own local gods. The ancient religions have their chief deity suffering an ordeal, dying and being reborn and this is no exception. The allegories of the Irish Lug and the Welsh Lleu have both survived for us to read. That of Lleu, for example, can be found in the *Mabinogion* as the fourth story, *Math, son of Mathonwy.* Therein we learn that Lleu Llaw Gyffes could not be killed. However, he was betrayed and killed by the only thing that could kill him – a magic spear that has been forged for a year and a day. However, Lleu was victorious over death and was resurrected as an eagle and flew away. He was searched for by his uncle Gwydion who found him sitting in the top of an oak tree. Every time the eagle shook himself, bits of flesh fell to the ground where they were devoured by a black sow.

This is but one association between the oak and the chief god, plus an association between oaks and sacrifices. Its Norse version has Odin hung on a tree sacrificing 'himself to himself.' In this case, the tree is not called an oak but has the name Yggdrasil. It is normally believed to be an ash tree, even though there are descriptions of it matching a yew tree. It is described as evergreen for example. However, being deciduous is important in the allegories because they 'die' each year at leaf-fall and come back to life again each spring at bud-burst. Lleu on the oak is in this phase between 'death' and new life. This is all part of the symbolism of that vast concept, The World Tree, found in mythologies worldwide. Common ideas run through them including small but significant details such as the Celtic deity being one-eyed and having special ravens, just as per Odin in Norse mythology.[6] In both cases prisoners of war were sacrificed to them in return for victory.[7]

The great festival of Lugh, (Lughnasadh -Festival of Lugh)[8] was at the beginning of August and to find a wealth of relevant material we need look no further than the Irish mythology/history. In Ireland 1st August is still called Lúnasa, after the god and this ancient celebration of Lu, and is still an important calendar date. Originally it was more than one day, for this was the time of for the great tribal assemblies of Ireland. The date is testimony to its antiquity for it is a cross-quarter day, falling exactly between the midsummer solstice and the autumn equinox, from when life on earth was seen as a reflection of the heavenly world above and the earthly calendar was synchronised with the movements of the heavenly bodies.

Birds of prey still raise our spirits as we watch them soar with such freedom and so it is not surprising that they became totem animals at a very early date. In due course the eagle was adopted by Christianity as the symbol of St. John the Evangelist, seen since the Middle Ages on many a Bible lectern, with wings raised, carrying the word of God on its back.

At this time they no doubt commemorated the sacrifice of Lugh on the oak tree but it was also a celebration of the harvest and therefore of the fulfilment of the fertility rituals earlier in the year when they anticipated new life arising out of death (see May Day references). As per usual, the arrival of Christianity had the Church accommodating such major events into its own calendar. Thus the celebration of Lugh became overlaid with that of St. Patrick, with the Croagh Patrick pilgrimage on the last Sunday in July. Other worthies in the pagan faith became the new Christian saints, some with names derived from Lug but all having their Catholic Feast Days at this time of the year, such as Láchtene on 1st August itself.

Highly important in this conversion process was the adoption of the pagan goddess Brigid as St. Brigid or Brigit. She was the goddess of all knowledge, plus fire and fertility and is believed by many to be so ancient that she goes back to the time when the Celts worshipped goddesses rather than gods. As goddess of fire and of fertility it looks as though she links with our oak quest and sure enough the early Christian shrines to St. Brigit were built under oak trees, as though supplanting her pagan shrines. That includes her famous retreat for holy women at Kildare in Leinster; (from *Cill Dara*, which means *church of the oak*). All men were excluded and indeed her whole cult had a female priesthood, perpetuating ancient times when all knowledge was safeguarded by women. The village woman skilled in the use of healing herbs has come down to modern times and the last echo of that today must be the midwife.

Brigit was held in higher esteem than Danu who was mother of the gods, with even the Druids (the Celtic caste responsible for knowledge) paying respect to Brigid as goddess of all knowledge. There is debate as to whether the word 'Druid' does or does not derive from an ancient word for oak. Those in favour say the first syllable comes from the ancient Greek for oak while the second syllable comes from the Sanskrit *vid* meaning knowledge. That will certainly fit in with what you will read in this little book but it does not mean that this is the true etymology of the word. Nevertheless, there is a long held association between Druids and oak groves where they held their meetings. In Britain the most famous story has Suetonius marching the Roman's troops up to Anglesey to destroy the sacred grove, to suppress the power of the Druids.

SHIPS CAME SAILING

We have a nasty little tendency to sort our knowledge into neat little compartments and so we can find text after text with the Iron Age ending with the invasion of the Romans in 43 CE. How absurd. The Romans did not conquer the whole of the British Isles and so the Iron Age culture continued in regions beyond Roman influence. Even where the Romans did establish themselves they did not wipe out the native British people. On the contrary, they needed them. For one thing, these people were very successful farmers and the Romans needed them to continue food production, to sustain themselves, the Romans, and to produce a surplus for export into the Roman Empire. We know that happened because archaeologists have now excavated so many Iron Age sites and found repeatedly that they did *not* come to an end with the arrival of the Romans, even in those places within close proximity of major Roman sites such as Peterborough. Thus a lot of Iron Age culture will have persisted right through the Roman period. That would be particularly true of ideas and beliefs including those that would be described as pagan by the Christians,[9] and they had arrived here during this period.

When the Romans departed in 410 CE they did not leave a spiritual void. More and more archaeological evidence is revealing that Christianity persisted. The Romans had never made it universal because they did not control the whole country. Roman Britain was a multi-cultural country, with differing faiths. Among the peoples were soldiers, traders and craftsmen from across the North Sea, from outside the Roman Empire, but adept at making a success of their lives in England. Some inevitably settled in order to further their trading businesses etc. and so came to raise their families here. They stayed on when Roman officialdom left, working with the Romanised Britons who stayed behind. More of these people crossed the sea to join them but it was a gradual process, spread over two hundred years or so. These were the people we learnt about as Angles, Saxons and Jutes. In other words, the Saxon conquests by the sword never happened. There never were mass migrations. That will upset a lot of traditionalists. Had it happened, archaeologists would find evidence of massacres, of farms and settlements burnt to the ground, and general interruptions to life on the sites being excavated. The old notion had the invading peoples driving the natives into the West Country and Wales which would mean a mass movement of perhaps one to two million people. You cannot shift that many without leaving any signs but the evidence is simply not there. On the contrary they find evidence of continuity, of a gradual assimilation of new peoples into the land.[10]

Out of this period of steady change came the notion of England, from Engleland or Angeln – the new lands of the Angles. The 'old' Angleland was in Denmark, in the southern portion of the Cimbric Penninsula, as far south as the River Elbe. South of that, from the Elbe to the Weser, was the territory of a confederation of tribes of Suebic descent that came to be known as 'Saxons'.[11] The Jutes came from the north of Denmark. Knowing these homelands is all very well but it has led to interpretation problems with archaeological finds. If, for example, a new pottery style occurs on a site it does not mean necessarily that new immigrants brought it or that they came from the locations just cited. The teenagers in the street outside enjoying their Japanese motorbikes are not themselves Japanese any more than a passing motorist in a BMW car is necessarily German. It is not people that move so much as ideas, designs and styles. These all move as freely as shared speech. That of course includes spiritual ideas and returns us to our quest for the sacred oak tree. All the peoples from the Continent came from cultures with great sky gods associated with the oak.

THE TUESDAY OAK

I only have to travel about twenty miles from here to the town of Godalming to drive along Tuesley Lane that runs over the hills above the town and drops down through the trees onto the level pasturelands that stretch towards Milford. This district is known as Tuesley, which takes its name from the great sky god Tiw (or Tig).[12] The name takes us back to the first Saxon settlers here who were still heathens and made a clearing or 'ley' on the hill for the rituals centred upon Tiw, which even in those days were ancient, since he is believed to be the same as the older sky god Tîwaz.

Tiw was a god of battle and combat and swordsmanship but the Saxon settlers probably kept those aspects in the back of their minds since they are believed to have arrived peacefully here in the upper Wey valley. Having chosen their location it was probably Tiw's concern for law and justice that was more important to them as they established a settlement. Probably that has grown into modern Godalming. If so then we might even know the name of the leader of those people, since the name Godalming is believed to derive from 'Godhelm's Ingas' - the lands of the people of Godhelm. That would fit nicely because *ingas* has been thought to denote very early settlements, possibly as far back as the 6th century. However, Godalming may not be quite that old. When archaeologists tried to correlate known heathen burial sites with *ingas* names they had to conclude that *ingas* comes into use a little later.[13] Nevertheless, up on the hill was the sacred site of Tiw, destroyed when Christians converted the heathens because this was where they built their new minster church. It was not very big. When excavated it was found to be 21 x 14 feet but just as the heathen site probably served as a cultural centre for a large territory, so the new Christian church was a minster or religious centre for a large district.[14] It had to be large because Saxon Surrey was thinly populated judging by the small amount of archaeological evidence found so far.[15]

Supplanting the old faith with the new must have been a major spiritual challenge since Tiw may also have been known as Saxnot or Seaxneat and if this is correct then he was one of the three greatest heathen gods to be overturned, judging by an early renunciation formula in the Vatican Library.[16] It specifies the renunciation of Wodan, Thunor and Saxnot. It was Saxnot who was the founder god of the royal dynasty of the East Saxons.[17]

His cult probably came from the lands between the Rhine and the Oder, which was the territory of the Semnones, later known as the Alimanni. Their king visited Rome in 92 CE and it was quite possibly from this visit that the Roman historian Tacitus gleaned information for his *Germania.* He tells us these people had a *Deus Regnator Omnium* or *God and Ruler of All* and although he gives us no other name this is most likely to have been Tîwaz (more likely than Wodan). He records that they had an annual ritual for themselves and the tribes to whom they were related and that this took place in a sacred wood, "*hallowed by the auguries of their forefathers and by ancient awe.*"[18] They could not enter it until they had been bound with a cord (for humility) and this 'binding' concept is widespread in ancient religions. So is another feature – Tîwaz had only one hand. That idea goes right back to the Bronze Age since rock engravings of that age in Scandinavia show a one-handed figure brandishing a weapon.

It seems, from the scant evidence available, that these people worshiped in the open air, in sacred groves, rather than in temple buildings. So although the stories of their gods lived on, giving us information about these people and their beliefs (albeit distorted later for entertainment value), we have precious few details about the rituals themselves. It is almost impossible to tell what it was like at Tuesley on a sacred day. We do not even know how often the site would have been used; presumably at least once a week on Tiw's sacred day. It is also likely that the spiritual leaders performed a daily office, towards the well-being of their community, even if the

community did not attend. Perhaps they kept a fire burning perpetually. We can find common threads running through the cultures from the Bronze and Iron Ages that remained so strong that the later Christians incorporated them. Thus we can conjecture that on a major ritual day the people followed a prescribed route of approach. How tempting it is to ponder whether this became Tuesley Lane. The name means a clearing so presumably the hillside remained wooded and the route led up through the trees until the people saw it opening up ahead of them. Did it all happen in the big 'field' like some evangelical meetings of our own age or did the grass encircle a sacred grove of oaks in the centre? We'll never know.

We can, however, imagine the people lining up to receive their ritual bonds before they could enter but even these may have been denied access to the very heart of the site, reserving that for the 'high priests'. We can imagine music too since that has been part of rituals since at least the Bronze Age. Almost certainly the spiritual leaders would have been under the influence of alcohol and hallucinogenic herbs, to enable them to commune with their god.[19] We don't know whether the assembled people also shared the brews that gave them a higher state of consciousness.[20] Although writers like Tacitus give us some information about the heathen tribes (albeit biased) there would have been differences between them and through time. If at Tuesley they still followed the reverences to Tîwaz as per the Semnones on the Continent then there would have been human sacrifice on the greatest day of the year (presuming Tacitus was told correctly) and the power of that was no doubt enhanced by the sound of drums and horns and other music. How that stirs our imaginations after so long a period of Christian symbolic representation of the sacrifice of Christ. Here the heathen Saxons had stark reality but maybe numbed by the use of toxic herbs as incense. The person to be sacrificed almost certainly had a last meal containing powerful herbs, as there was an ancient tradition for that. Certainly there is nothing in the literature or in the archaeology to suggest that these people died in fear. Fear of death came with the Christians and their concepts of Judgement Day and perpetual damnation in the fires of hell. The heathens were portrayed as barbaric by Tacitus but he and his readership considered that as Romans, they were far superior to the 'primitive' peoples on the northern fringe of their Empire. These were people of a different culture but to think of them as 'barbaric' would be to underestimate them severely. Their religion and culture had very sophisticated metaphysics. Their god Tiw was a god of the sword but he not only wielded one in battle but also in judgement, upon those criminals condemned to capital punishment. In other words, they had law and order and justice. That's not my idea of 'barbaric'. So although they had been a warring people, who practised capital punishment, they came to Tuesley to start a new and settled life, tilling the soil and suckled their sons, knowing that each would one day be initiated into the cult of the great sky god who had given them so much. His roles would in due course be subsumed into those of gods with different names, like Woden and Thor, but his importance has been perpetuated in the name of his sacred day each week. That is Mardi to the French because Tiw shared characteristics with Mars, the Roman god of war, but in England we stuck to the original Tiw and have Tuesday.

THE WEDNESDAY OAK

The shadows of two black ravens passed over the country each day. At nightfall they returned to the lands beyond, to the great hall of their master, where they reported back all their sightings. They ensured he remained 'all-knowing' for he was Odin, the supreme god. He sat in his great high chair, feet up on his footstool, sipping his mead from a magnificent horn, and listened intently to the reports from his raven agents, Huginn (thought) and Muninn (memory). As the 'all-seeing' god he should have got up and had a look for himself but he could be a wee bit indolent. After all, from where he sat his eye could reach the furthest depths of all the worlds. Even so, the other gods criticised his sloth and he could make man anxious with his unreliability. Nevertheless, to the Norse peoples he was their father god, known as Allfather.

When spurred into action he rolled out across the skies in his wondrous chariot drawn by an eight-legged horse, Sleipnir. You have heard it go by and thought it was thunder! You have seen it too - in the northern night sky where seven prominent stars make up the 'Chariot of Odin'[21] (The Great Bear, The Plough). The differences

make no difference. We are dealing with great sky gods, associated with thunderstorms and thereby with oak trees. They burst into leaf in April, when the constellation is best seen, and when it was believed that Odin stirred himself after the winter. The Vikings did the same and prepared themselves for another summer's adventuring. They had one of their year's great festivals which is described in the *Ynglinga* Saga as '*in summer, for victory*'. Odin, as the god of war and bringer of victory, went adventuring with them.[22]

He came to England and has given rise to numerous place names, under his various aliases, (he has over 200 of them) but in earliest times he seems to have evolved out of Tiwaz. Evidence suggests that the name change occurred at about the 5th century. In the Saxon homeland he became Wodan. Over here they called him Woden. To the Vikings and Danes he was Odin. When the Romans heard about him they recognised characteristics shared with their god Mercury and under that name is how they wrote about him. Thus his sacred day became *mercredi* to the French. The English kept Woden, as in Woden's Day or Wednesday.

The faith in Odin prepared the people for the stories of the Christian missionaries; for example, Odin hanging from a tree as a sacrifice to himself parallels Christ's Crucifixion, even down to the detail of them both having their side pierced with a spear. Archaeology has proven the Odin version predates Christianity. Such forms of sacrifice are far older and arose independently of Christianity even if they later blurred in people's minds. Thus the famous Saxon poem *The Dream of the Rood* portrays Christ as a Saxon warrior-king, just as the *Hávamál* presents Odin as a father-god who suffers and overcomes death. It was the work of the early Christian missionaries to convert allegiance from Odin to the new god but at least many basic concepts were in place already.

If we ask what it would have been like at a festival in honour of Odin, we are stuck for information. Of course it suited the Romans to report that there were human sacrifices since they wanted to brand the people barbaric but writers within the culture record it too. After all, to them, it was right and proper. From the 11th century we hear from Adam of Bremen[23] that at the great temple at Uppsala male slaves (and male animals) were sacrificed and hanged from the trees. This ritual was performed only every nine years. Prisoners of war were dispatched immediately. As need arose, offerings were made to attract the god's attention in order to try and change circumstances. From two sources, the *Gautreks Saga* and from the 12th century Danish historian Saxo Grammaticus, we hear of the same event : Vikar, king of the Vikings was becalmed at sea and prayed to Odin for a wind but realised that somebody on board would need to be sacrificed as an offering in return. When they drew lots to decide who to sacrifice it was the king himself who drew the fatal lot and was duly hanged from the mast. Kings were not exempt from religious practice. They were deemed to rule by divine will and if things went wrong it was judged that the gods had withdrawn their goodwill, so the people would dispatch their unholy king and start again. That lot fell upon two Swedish kings, Domalde and Olof Trätälja, who were sacrificed when extended famine was interpreted as divine displeasure. The same system operated in England too. When St. Wilfrid landed in Sussex the South Saxons were about to sacrifice their king to release their kingdom from famine. Famines were suffered regularly in England, with the *Anglo-Saxon Chronicles* recording over fifty of the severest. Killing the king was the last resort, after performing fertility rituals again and then sacrificing lesser mortals. Deviations from this norm were evidently viewed with misgivings, as in the story of the Swedish king Aun who claimed receiving a holy assurance that he could extend his life by sacrificing one of his sons every ten years. He did that nine times but when it came to his tenth and final son the people intervened. The story is of course mythological,[24] from the explanation of how Sweden and its provinces came into being. Our earliest literature is a wonderful blend of the real and the mythical. Some people have wondered whether even Odin himself was once an ancient mortal leader so famed that he became deified just as we can debate whether there was ever a real King Arthur or a real Jesus Christ.

THE THURSDAY OAK

A few miles from Tuesley lies the village of Thursley, folded smartly into the landscape, below the Devil's Punch Bowl and Gibbet Hill. The very names stir the imagination and mine was certainly stirred back in 1963, when I was taken into the church and shown two little windows punctured through the north wall of the chancel. They were Saxon and still retained their Saxon oak window frames, which the guide said were the only survivors in Britain. I was writing, most grudgingly, a school project on the uses of British trees and showing me these little frames was supposed to inspire me. They certainly did, as I was made to imagine the Saxon priest standing where I was

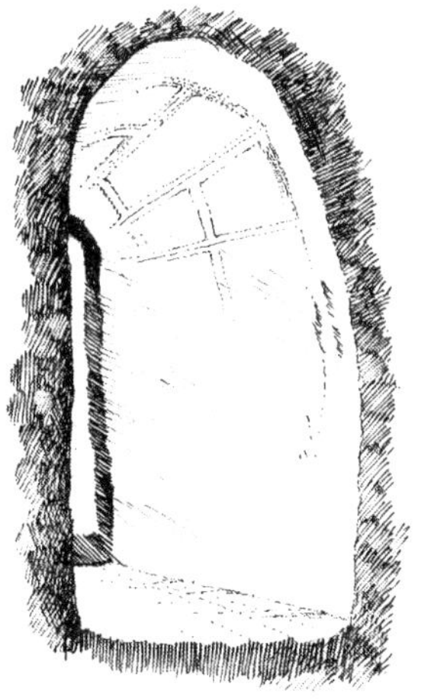

One of the two little Saxon windows in the north wall of the chancel in Thursley parish church. The 'mortar lines' were added in red paint, as a decoration, by the Normans.

standing, looking out onto a world of residual paganism, a world peopled by those who had accepted the new faith and yet knew also the beliefs of the old. In particular they would have known about Thor since their village of Thursley was named after him – the 'ley' or clearing of Thor.

As we left we paused to look up at the village sign (since stolen). There was Thor, complete with his famous hammer and all around us were his sacred oak trees. Those little windows had certainly opened up a new world for me – or should I say door? The word for 'oak' and for 'door' is the same or similar in ancient languages, from Irish and Welsh to Greek and back into far older languages. How odd that so many different cultures should all choose to associate the two, unless there was a common cultural link. That could be the idea of the oak being the door to the Otherworld. It would certainly link with Thor. Bolts of lightning striking oak trees were messages from Thor as he bridged the gap between mortal earth and the Otherworlds. So I walked on, trying to imagine that here in an oak wood had been a sacred site dedicated to Thor. It would help explain why Thursley is so placed in the landscape, for although the church stands on a ridge above a watercourse, it does seem today that there are plenty of other such sites in the rumpled landscape. Why did they choose this particular spot? Was it crowned with a group of wonderful spreading oaks, all green and mossy, which were viewed as a sign from Thor?

So who was this Thor? He was another sky god, associated with lightning and oak trees. It was the Norse who called him Thor while the Saxons called him Thunor or Thonar. Thus in south west Surrey we find Thursley while in south east Surrey there is Thunderfield at Horley. He was venerated widely and when the place-name enthusiasts plotted his connections they noticed that all those places where the name suggests a sacred site are in southern England settled by the Saxons. There are none in the Midlands and North where the Angles settled. That is not to say the Angles had never heard of him, only that we have no place-names suggesting a veneration site. There are plenty of Thor names in Anglian regions but they are believed to derive from personal names, from where the Danes had named their sons after him; there is an abundance of such names in that part of England governed as the Danelaw. As usual there is a snag. The old word for giant or demon was *thyrs* and so presumably this is reflected in some place-names without us knowing.

Thunor is believed to have evolved out of Donar, an earlier Germanic god of thunder and lightning, who was also symbolised with an axe or a hammer. The holy day of the week for that god gave rise to the modern German Donnerstag for Thursday, which is of course Thor's day in our modern weekdays. When the Romans encountered these cultures they identified the god with their own god of thunder and lightning, Jupiter or Jove, hence 'dies Jovis' or 'Jove's Day'. Donar was associated also, in Roman minds, with Hercules who wielded a club just as Donar and Thor each wielded their mighty hammer. In due course Thunor/Thor became mightier than Woden/Odin. It is accepted generally that Thor was believed to be the son of Odin.[25]

He features prominently in the stories of old but of course these are just that – stories. So often they must have been recorded for their entertainment value and by Christian writers at that, so it is highly unlikely that they give us a true insight into the old faiths. There are language problems too. The word 'temple' brings to our minds a building although the word means a 'sanctuary or sacred space' and therefore can mean a sacred *open* space like an oak grove, and the distinction is not always clear in the old writings. The transition from grove to building cannot be dated precisely but by the late period there were temples of Thor that were buildings. There was a sacred use of fire and light and that could only have been really effective inside a dark building. Those who entered found there was a statue of the god and if the temple was dedicated to several gods then Thor was given pre-eminence. At their best these sculptures were life-size or larger – one late saga says,

"Thor sat in the middle. He was the most highly honoured. He was huge, and all adorned with gold and silver. Thor was arranged to sit in a chariot; he was very splendid. There were goats, two of them, harnessed in front of him, very well wrought. Both car and goats ran on wheels. The rope around the horns of the goats was of twisted silver, and the whole was worked with extremely fine craftsmanship."[26]

The two goats, Tanngniost and Tanngrisnir, are crucial to the iconography of Thor. When they drew this chariot of the thunder god across the skies mortals said it was thundering. Interestingly the whole sculpture was mounted on wheels and the implication in the full story is that by pulling it along mortals were rendering service to Thor. Surely this implies that on highly sacred days this sculpture was rolled out and became the focal point of the procession – just as the Roman Catholic Church in some places parades a giant statue of the Blessed Virgin Mary out of the Cathedral and through the gathered crowds. Perhaps this gives us an insight into what it would have been like at a major ritual in honour of Thor.

I would love to have seen the craftsmanship that impressed the writer so much. Nothing on this scale was allowed to survive once Christianity took over but we do know from smaller artefacts that these people had superb skills at both design and execution. This is not the work of barbarians but of a sophisticated culture with a highly developed appreciation of beauty. That in itself was surely drawn from the natural world, where a jeweller could be inspired by dew drops on coloured petals sparkling in the rising sun. I do not believe for one minute those writers who describe these people as living in a dark world of fear, where the northern forests were full of evil spirits. That is Christian prejudice. It is not reflected in the original texts, which leave us concluding that the finest heathen temple buildings must have been richly ornamented, with intricately carved woodwork emboldened by painters and gilders. Perhaps the fact that there were Christian directives to convert pagan temples into churches implies that these were *worthy* of the new dedication. They tell us also that the design was suitable: a communal space that would become the church nave and perhaps an extension that became the chancel but certainly a reserved space that would become the sanctuary. That's where the sculptures stood. Thor's was made from one of his sacred oaks and could be larger than life-size. Robes are mention in some of the references and there's an intriguing line in an 11th century Irish Christian poem where the king of Dublin is told to take '*the golden castle from the hands of the black devil.*' This has been interpreted[27] as removing gold from the idol but was 'black' used simply to signify evil (from a Christian viewpoint) or was it also imagery of oak blackened by the smoke from tallow lamps? Many references testify to the idol being adorned with gold and In particular there was a gold (or silver) ring upon which oaths were sworn. A ring was taken from the Dublin temple by King Maelseachlainn in 994 whereby the Christian king removed the means by which heathens could swear allegiance to their god.[28] In addition to precious metals there was a sacred base metal – iron. They could strike sparks (lightning) from the iron to light a sacred fire. Some references infer that an iron nail was driven into the head (as was practised long after by the Scride Finnus – Lapps of Finland) while others refer to iron nails being in the great oak pillars of the sanctuary structure. A late saga records that the altar was topped with iron because upon this was burned a perpetual fire.[29] So the altar was not of stone but of wood and that too must have been of oak. Certainly of oak was the 'high seat'. Thor's sculpture was flanked by carved pillars and was presumably of a sitting figure or perhaps in some cases the high back of the seat terminated in the image.[30] Wherever the concept of the all-important seat came from it has persisted right down to the present, with the leader of a group being the chairman, chair-person or chair, while a professor holds the chair of his subject in his university seat of learning, and so forth.

These images and practices travelled afar. There is an interesting story from Scandinavia where 9th century Norway was composed of little sub-kingdoms until Harald Fairhair united them by conquest and ruled over them (872-933) as the first king of all Norway. It was not an easy time and on the little island of Most one man, Thorolf Mostrarskegg, decided it might be better to emigrate to Iceland. He consulted Thor and was soon packing his ship to leave. He dismantled Thor's shrine, including the high seat pillars, and loaded them on his ship together with soil he had taken from under Thor's seat. On approaching Iceland, Thorolf threw overboard the high-seat pillars so that Thor could guide them ashore and thereby indicate where he wanted Thorolf to settle.[31] All went well and soon Thorolf was building a new home, assembling Thor's shrine again, and marking the boundary of his new property with fire.[32] In our own time it was still the practice to burn out evil and ensure fertility in the Severn Valley orchards by running round the boundary dragging a burning faggot, albeit for fun, along with wassailing the fruit trees.

AXEING THE OAK

To sketch this scene I went down to the South Downs to the Iron Age hill-fort at the Trundle, overlooking Chichester with its cathedral spire and the Sussex coastal plain. The view disappeared into the heat haze but on clearer days you can see the inlets of the sea on the right and the Solent beyond and the Isle of Wight beyond that. The odd name of Wight comes from Wightgar who ruled the Jutes. He held the island and southern Hampshire to the west and Kent to the east but the South Saxons held on to their kingdom in the middle. They also remained loyal to their traditional beliefs, making this the last pagan landscape in Saxon England. It was in Kent of course that Christianity is said to have started, when Pope Gregory sent St. Augustine in 595/96. In fact there were Christians in the country already and Augustine's mission was about converting the remaining pagans and, to establish an *organised* Church, in line with Roman practice. Evangelising the landscape above was the work not of Augustine but St. Wilfrid, who arrived in 681. I wondered whether this is the landscape where the sacred oaks got their final axeing.

Wilfrid had been banished from Northumbria and denied refuge by both Mercia and Wessex but when he turned to Sussex, to King Aethelwealh and Queen Eaba, they allowed him to stay. Aelthelwealh had only recently been converted and baptised in Mercia by King Wulfhere who became his godfather, while Queen Ebba came from a Christian family in the kingdom of the Hwiccas.[33] The royal house was therefore Christian but the rest of the South Saxon kingdom was still pagan. Wilfrid was allowed to evangelise and it was agreed that he could baptise the leaders while his monks were allowed to baptise the rest of the people. It was an important day and so of course it rained! That was wonderful because it broke a three year drought that had brought famine to the kingdom. They had gone through their usual pagan practices to bring rain but to no avail and were considering their final option – sacrificing their king.[34] Then along comes Wilfrid promising salvation for all, famine or not, and so they took up his option.

That the king and his people were descended from the gods was crucial because our usual understanding is that if the king changed allegiance from one god to another he took his people with him automatically. That obviously had not happened in Sussex but it does explain the achievement of Augustine in Kent when he converted King Ethelbert[35] and *all of Kent*. That could otherwise leave us wondering how a few evangelists could race round Kent baptising everybody so successfully and so very fast. Inducting the people into the new faith did of course take time but made all the easier by it having practically no concepts that were unfamiliar to the people in the pagan faiths. The main difference was the *guarantee* of salvation to all true believers – or suffer eternal damnation. That threat introduced fear into death. Secondly, there were many Christians established already in the country.

To explore around this idea a little further let us turn back to the sketch from The Trundle overlooking Chichester. The city is a Roman foundation that was called Noviomagus Reginorum which translates as 'New Market of the Kingdom'. That would have been of the late Iron Age kingdom, for which there were settlements and ports all around this coastline with its deep inlets. The Romans were accepted into the area and set up a local head quarters at Fishbourne.[36] They allowed the British to continue their heathen practices, including reverence for the sky gods and their oaken lightning tree, now married up with similar Roman beliefs. The new Roman market is thought to have replaced an older one down at Selsey. It continued to function after the official departure of the Roman administration and so became the royal centre for the new South Saxon kingdom of Sussex, established by Ella, a heathen. It was this royal house that accepted Wilfrid. Thus there is a continuity of thinking and heathen religious belief right through these centuries.

Some pagan kingdoms, like the East Saxons, converted to the new faith only to have their king return them to the old faiths for a while.[37] The new religion succeeded overall, in part at least, because it was organised and had a central control to hold it all together. When Wilfrid set up his cathedral at Selsey he was perpetuating Roman administration for by the late Roman Empire there were so many provinces that they were grouped into a larger unit called a diocese. That is what the Roman Church took over in the 5th and 6th centuries and today the definition of diocese is explained entirely in Church terms. While all this was happening the old faiths persisted in parallel. Outside of Britain they were still flourishing, with important temples as far flung as Dublin and Upsalla, until the 10th century and later.

As I sketched the view from the Trundle I was thinking there were probably more trees than when they built the Roman Palace at Fishbourne. It must have been nearly all corn fields then. Turning round, the view north has always been over the great oak forest of the Weald. Just below sits the little village of Singleton with its Saxon church. I went to see it and approached up narrow ‘streets’ that must survive from when the Saxon builders trundled their materials that way. Some of the stone had been brought across from the Isle of Wight so they obviously took the enterprise seriously but I did wonder how many of them were entirely Christian. Certainly they would have known the stories about the old gods because they are so entertaining and often humorous. It is not difficult to imagine those workmen telling stories under cover while they waited for the rain to ease, dipping their bread into a pot of broth. Somebody left a pot behind. It is on display in the church.

So there was a continuity of pagan belief through all these times, which worried Christian missionaries. Augustine himself wrote back to his boss and asked Pope Gregory what he should do about the English hanging up evergreens at Christmas as per their fertility rituals at the winter solstice. The Church had already superimposed the celebration of Christ's birth upon the date of this pagan practice and so Gregory told Augustine to Christianise the practice. Thus the Christmas holly became the sacred body of Christ and the English were allowed Christmas decorations by papal authority. The old rituals were, however, two-part. They crowned the winter king/god, as the holly king, at the winter solstice but he was the successor of the summer king crowned at the summer solstice, and he was the oak king. The Church adopted that as the Feast Day of St. John the Baptist, because he heralded the coming of Christ six months beforehand.[38] The pagans celebrated at this time the fulfilment of their mid-winter fertility rituals and so all manner of flowers and crops and trees were used, with oak in a prominent position of course. These got Christianised as the 'Herbs of St. John' of which the one commemorated by name is St. John's Wort. In post-Reformation Protestant England this Church festival declined but is still important in many European Catholic countries.

Allegiance to the oak remained great and so people were soon understanding that Christ's Cross was made of oak, rationalised by the knowledge that the timber is very heavy and Christ stumbled under the weight of his Cross on the road to Calvary.[39] It represents more than that though, for it was been noted already that the oak was the tree of sacrifice in allegories of the sky gods, making this Christian version easy to assimilate. It became the new focal point. The notion of pagan 'tree worship' is ridiculous if it is taken to mean that people worshipped the tree *as a god.* The tree was the focus of worship in just the same way as Christians do not worship the Cross but focus upon it as a potent symbol of their Faith. They wear an amulet of the Cross around their necks just as the pagans wore amulets of Thor's hammer, and it is thought that some people at conversion time wore both. Archaeologists have unearthed a mould in which both could be cast at the same time.

A great crucifix or rood became the focal point in the Christian churches and these too were made of oak. One such church survives in England, at Greenstead-juxta-Ongar in Essex. It has been judged to be 8th or 9th century but recent dendochronology counts give it a mid-11th century date of about the time of the Norman invasion.[40] The walls are created from oak trunks split in half and lined up side by side, with the split surfaces forming the continuous plane of the inner wall, while the outer wall has been left as a line of bulging trunks. The Church continued with traditional building practices and so if we can't see more than one building we can see thousands of medieval roofs, doors, etc. plus all the wonderfully carved fittings: rood and chancel screens, parclose screens, bench-ends, font covers pulpits, cathedral choir stalls, etc. – all worked in oak.

The illustrations here are from two of the misericords in the stalls at Lingfield, Surrey. Although all the fittings and furnishings are oaken for practical reasons they also perpetuate the spiritual allegiance to the tree: the tree that offers the best service to God. This is particularly so when carved and painted to illustrate the faith. Of particular interest to this study are the images, whether in wood or stone, that are known as the Green Man.

THE GREEN MAN

For any readers who have yet to be touched by the modern enthusiasm for the 'Green Man', it is a facial image with either foliage emanating from the mouth or else wreathing/creating the face in a mask-like fashion.[41] Such imagery reached the height of popularity during medieval times but there is evidence of its existence centuries earlier. Each version is different and all are a great mystery. No contemporary written reference has been found to any of the old ones in Britain and there are many hundreds surviving today and countless more must have been destroyed at the Reformation. Consequently we have no certain knowledge as to their meaning, which has led to widely differing speculations. I like my thinking to start with the evidence and that is how this section will proceed.

Example from Winchelsea, Sussex. 14th century.
The under-cutting of the oak is quite remarkable, and the rendering of the knobbly twigs acutely accurate, while the leaves are so detailed it is possible to determine that he copied a piece of Quercus robur rather than Quercus petraea.

The name Green Man, written with capital initials, was first applied to them in 1939 by Lady Raglan[42] when she realised how many there were and that they must be significant. Hitherto they had appeared in architectural descriptions simply as 'foliated heads' etc. The image lends itself to fine design and the medieval craftsmen often demonstrated their skills to the utmost upon them, so not only are they mysterious but the best are very beautiful and have never lost their appeal.[43]

The recent enthusiasm for these leafy heads has led to their adoption by many 'green' factions. Although this is an interesting, development, it is going to lead us off the main theme of this little book. Instead, let us start by looking at the medieval design. It is simple and therefore immediately recognisable but part of this recognition relies upon there being nothing else like it, so it can be argued that it must have carried an important message/meaning. That meaning is invariably conveyed by a male image *but* there are many where it is no longer possible to distinguish the gender. There are plenty of bestial versions too. The foliage can be found most often emanating from the mouth but there are plenty of examples where it can be found growing out of the nostrils, ears, and face or wreathed around the head. Invariably the face is rendered below/behind the foliage so that the growth becomes foremost in the message.

Their positioning in the church tells us a lot. They are everywhere! They must be expressing a universal truth of the religious beliefs of the faith (in medieval times in this section). There are fewer in the chancel and sanctuary parts of the church[44] but this is hardly surprising seeing as these areas were reserved for the priests. The fact that the Green Man *does* occur in chancels is crucial for refuting suggestions that these images are in some way 'evil'. In the iconography of the medieval church the chancel represented Heaven; we can walk into the little Sussex church of Hardham next to Pulborough and there find a complete set of 12th century wall paintings, showing this heavenly aspect, with Christ in Glory, the Apostles and the Church Elders etc. There can be no evil in Heaven because St. Michael cast it out:

And there was war in heaven: Michael and his angels fought against the dragon; and the dragon fought and his angels, and prevailed not; neither was their place found any more in heaven.

(Book of Revelation 12, 7-8; AV)

Although the motif does not represent evil as such, it is almost certainly a Christianised version of an older pagan idea and to some people any faith that is not Christian is inherently evil, whatever concept it expresses. That the Green Man comes out of pagan times has been refuted on the grounds that these images do not occur in English churches until Norman times. No carved Saxon version survives in Britain and that must be significant.[45] Wait a minute; there are only a handful of near-complete Saxon churches to look at and none retains any decorative scheme. Even loose or re-used sculptures are rare. Surely it is a bit rash to conclude the image was unknown to the Saxons.[46] On the contrary, the Saxons must surely have known it well simply because the Normans used it abundantly, as though they expected recognition. All that the Church had to do was to accept the pagan image and update its meaning. So what pagan practices were still popular all over the country in the later 12th century and early 13th century?

Thoughts must turn to 'Bringing in the May'. The Church railed against the continuance of such practices; for which the earliest surviving text[47] is from about 1240 when Roberte Grosseteste, Bishop of Lincoln, condemned his priests for demeaning themselves by enjoying '*games which they call the bringing-in of May.*'[48] It had become a great holiday but previously had been a serious celebration, when the new growth of spring was seen as a fulfilment of the fertility rituals performed earlier in the year. It was a reassurance that there was going to be another harvest time. The people would not abandon that event for fear of famine, so the Christian Church had to accept it. There would have been regional variations but from these the most famous conversion was of the celebrations of the fertility goddess Oestre into Easter for celebrating the Resurrection of Christ. That raises interesting interpretation possibilities, without forcing the evidence to fit a theory.

Firstly, we know that people originally celebrated out in the woods, until early Christian rulers like King Cnut outlawed it. The people got round that by going out before dawn and gathered armfuls of new greenery which they brought back! This was 'Bringing in the May'. We can picture them in church, faces peering excitedly through armfuls of twigs, just like the Green Man image.[49] Is this what we see among the sculptures (c.1290) in the Chapter House at Southwell Minster, Notts., where two hands hold a loop of hawthorn around the face?[50] The hawthorn is known still as 'May' or 'May Blossom' and was Christianised as an emblem of the Blessed Virgin Mary. Quite possibly these celebrations involved drama with dressing up, as they did on Corpus Christi Day etc. Look along the choir stalls in Winchester Cathedral and in one of the spandrels is a Green Man figure (rather than just the face) with a sword in one hand and a small round shield in the other. He is not in knight's gear but dressed in the usual medieval tunic, including the sort of hat worn by other entertainers illustrated in medieval art. Is he an actor?

Secondly, there are clues in the image that the Church was using it as part of the faith in the Resurrection. Look at the leaves. The early ones are stylised but even then nearly always indented or lobed.[51] Later the style veers towards realism and then we can actually identify the species of plant the artists had in mind. Just two species dominate - oak and vine – both with lobed/indented leaves. It was so important that these should be recognised as such that the artists tended to add the acorns and grapes for good measure. Surely that must be significant, especially when both carry the same symbolism, and both associate with the concept of resurrection. We have noted already that the ancient religions had a three-part belief in the deity suffering an ordeal, dying and being reborn and that this was associated with oak trees because they 'die' each year at leaf-fall and come back to life again each spring at bud-burst. The Christian Church would have had no trouble accommodating that, alongside its own symbol of the Resurrected Christ – the vine.

There are carvings that show this. Let us consider three examples on bench-ends in the Somerset churches at Bicknoller, Lyng and Barwick. All three have the Green Man at the base and the vine scrolling upwards from their mouths before entwining so as to provide a perch for a phoenix as symbol of the Resurrection. It is immediately recognisable at Lyng and Barwick because of the traditional raised but half-folded wings and these two help us understand the Bicknoller bird which looks much like any other in medieval carving. In its beak it is holding a vine shoot that does not terminate in the usual bunch of grapes but in a poppy pod; the poppy symbolising sleep and death.

At the 12th century church at Sutton Benger in Wiltshire there is this magnificent Green Man carving (*illus. below*). In all probability this is Victorian work as it could hardly have survived so unscathed for centuries and it does not match the other medieval carving there. However, it could be a reworking of a medieval image and likely to be so with a third tree included and that is the hawthorn.

For as long as we can tell, the hawthorn has been used in fertility rituals, hence 'bringing in the May'. Many people still call it 'May blossom' and some will admit that after pollination the flowers smell of sex. It was probably that smell that turned this tree into the prime sacred tree for the festival. The Roman Catholic Church could not break people's allegiance to it and so it got adopted as the symbol of

Barwick

Bicknoller

Lyng

the Virgin Mary – the closest they had to a mother goddess of fertility. We know the lobed leaves in the carvings are hawthorn because the fruits have been rendered. Even more significantly, some little birds (?greenfinches) are shown pecking at the fruit – attacking the fruit of the Virgin Mary which was Christ. This makes the carving all encompassing, with the Green Man reminding men in particular of Christ's Passion while the women of the parish are reminded of the torment suffered by the Virgin Mary at this time. Ultimately it is the Christian promise of everlasting life through a belief in Jesus Christ – the age-old cycle of life, death and rebirth.

Approach to Gloucester Cathedral; look for the Green Man in the bosses of the porch and there are other examples around the building.

GOSPEL OAKS

It is said, sometimes, that the name Gospel Oak derives from Christianity being preached to the Saxon heathens beneath them or that they grow where Christians felled one of Odin's sacred oaks. It is far more likely that these are the sites where the Gospels were liberated from their Latin and preached in English for the first time – and to imagine that we need to dress our congregation in late medieval costume.

They had to meet well away from village centres because there was there was fierce opposition from the Church, and the secular authorities that backed them, to any attempt to put the faith into the common tongue. They feared it would lose its magical hold, its mystery, its power – and the Church officers would have their social position diminished. The Gospels in English were preached well away from the village church, under great oaks, right out on the parish boundary. Oak trees had long been used as boundary markers and by meeting on the boundary, spilling into two parishes, it was not clear which authority should take responsibility, and thereby the cost and effort of enforcing the law. It has always been better if things go wrong on somebody else's patch!

To explore this further we only have to look at the life and times of John Wycliffe and the Lollards. I only have to go a mile or so into Addlestone and there's 'Wycliffe's Oak'. Today it is known as The Crouch Oak, at the northern end of Crouch Oak Lane. It is on the boundary of Windsor Park and measuring its girth to calculate its age by Alan Mitchel's formula gives a very late Saxon date. It would not have had heathens under its boughs because it was a mere stripling in those days and the district had been Christianised long before with the founding of nearby Chertsey Abbey in 666 CE. By tradition it did hear John Wycliffe preaching. Maybe it was one of those days when Wycliffe denounced the Church for interfering with temporal affairs and for owning temporal possessions. The villagers would have loved that. Probably they were a bit shocked when he denounced the doctrine of transubstantiation but they wanted to know more. They needed to be able to read the scriptures for themselves. If he was going to organise the translation of the Bible from Latin into English they were not going to complain. The Pope was livid.

Crouch Oak

Wycliffe died in 1384 and was buried at Lutterworth in Leicestershire, where he was rector, but in 1428 the Bishop of Lincoln had his bones dug up and burnt. Four hundred years later, Wycliffe was held in respect again and with the approach of the anniversary in 1828 there were letters in *The Times* proposing a monument should be erected at Lutterworth. That brought a letter from 'WB' that the monument should be in Addlestone: *I think, therefore, that the best monument to the memory of that great man would be, to erect a church upon the scene of his former labours.'* What ! Cut down the Crouch Oak ! That was not allowed. This was all local politics anyway. Addlestone was part of Chertsey and 'WB' was urging that it should be carved off and given separate parish status but he would have to wait eight years for that, and the building of St. Paul's parish church in 1836. Some locals saw this as further entrenchment of the Establishment and so in 1828 they *did* build a church in Crouch Oak Lane but it was definitely not for the Church of England. It was Nonconformist![52]

It was the Nonconformist movements in the 17th century onwards that re-invented outdoor evangelising with preachers like John Wesley attracting crowds in their thousands. Many of the Gospel Oaks must date from such events. By then the country was Protestant and the reformed Church had turned its back upon ritual and turned instead towards a greater simplicity with the emphasis firmly upon the word of god. The old illustrations in the church, whether carved or painted or rendered in glass, had in most cases been destroyed or whitewashed over. Only a small fraction survives today. Without the imagery it is difficult to continue the veneration of the oak in religious terms. This esteemed tree now becomes important in the secular landscape and held people's emotions through its natural beauty. With the ending of the Civil Wars and the Restoration of the monarchy in 1660 many a landowner had to recover his wealth and reconstitute his country park. The man who preached this gospel was John Evelyn, first by giving a lecture to the Royal Society in 1662 on the beauty and economic value of planting trees and then publishing a big book on the subject in 1664 – *Silva: or a Discourse of Forest-Trees, and the Propagation of Timber in His Majesty's Dominions*. Park after Park was landscaped and planted up with trees and just one of John Evelyn's designs survives, at Albury Park in Surrey. When we read the planting lists in surviving records we find the thousands of oaks were used and of course the trend has not finished yet. Oak is still the most frequently planted amenity tree today. We hold it very much as the great symbol of England. After the Great Storm in 1987 that destroyed several millions of trees across southern England there was a massive replanting scheme. The Queen and her Barons met at Runnymede, by the Magna Carta site (*Illus. below*), and planted trees. Of course they planted oaks ! We have no other great symbol of England for such a famous site – Good Old English Oak – forgetting the French have good old French oak and the Germans have good old German oak !

HEAVEN PRESERVE US

There is another strand to this quest that runs parallel. As we have seen, our far distant ancestors saw the oak not only as a link with the gods but representing the knowledge handed down to us by those gods. In particular, the success or failure of herbalism was seen very much as being dependent upon them. The best medicines came from the sacred herbs or perhaps that should be that the best herbs were deemed sacred? Either way, the two were entwined. Christianity did not change that directly. It asserted that all plants were created by God on the third day of Creation and that he commanded them to bear fruit – all plants were to have a purpose and a value. Therefore, pagan herbalism was allowed to continue, although it tactfully or faithfully updated the wording of incantations to exchange names of pagan deities for Christian ones (or used both).

Reading their 'leechbooks' today we do of course find prescriptions containing oak. The earliest surviving English medical treatise[53] is probably from the mid 9th century. Therein we read of oak in a herbal bath: "*Make him a good bath, too: apple, thorn, blackthorn, ash, quickbeam, oak, boarthroat, elecampane, bishopwort, ivy, betony, ribwort, radish. Boil this all in water and this is a good bath against thigh-ache.*"[54] Oak was probably included here for its astringent qualities, as in another recipe for bites, that occurs in what is known as Bald's *Leechbooks*. This three-part work was probably compiled at the Winchester scriptorium about 950 CE and is therefore likely to be the oldest complete medical treatise in English[55] Apart from exploiting the active ingredients for treatments, oak has also been used for amulets to ward off problems in the first place, as found in a Saxon woman's grave at Fonaby, Lincolnshire, where it was attached to the woman's girdle.[56]

This notion that the sacred oak would provide protection led to whole houses being built around them, such as at Cawdor Castle and the Old Manor House at Knaresborough while another at Huntingfield in Suffolk was built around not one but six oak trees. This practice has led Pollington to query[57] whether it connects with the Scandinavian *barnstokker* (baby/tree trunk) which was seen as "*a potent symbol of regeneration of the family.*" It was the custom at a wedding for the groom to slash such a tree with his sword and to read from the gash the future of the marriage, while women suffering a difficult childbirth would evoke or clasp such trees for aid. Ancient healing was a wonderful amalgam of practical and spiritual and that had to stay in use right through the Middle Ages because Christianity kerbed the development of medicine, until the advent of Protestantism.

In particular Christianity curtailed intrusive medicine. It viewed ill health as a punishment or trial from God and therefore it was impertinent at the least to try and interfere with that. Similarly, the human body was one of the wonders of Creation and to open one up and investigate its anatomy was gross impertinence, so surgery was rare and limited. Consequently there were very few medieval hospitals and even those were run by the church, such as St. Bartholomew's in London. The doctors and nurses were ranked lower than the priests so the emphasis was upon spiritual healing above physical healing. It was one of the Seven Deeds of Mercy to tend the sick, but that tending was basically first aid, to relieve some of the suffering but not going so far as to interfere with God's punishment or trial. That said, modern archaeology is coming up with some unexpected finds, indicating that the above principles were not adhered to as vigilantly as the fundamentalists would have liked.

Protestantism in England and Holland broke the taboos and by the 17th century there were great advances in medical practice, e.g. William Harvey proved the circulation of the blood and Rembrandt was able to paint Dr. Tulp dissecting for an anatomy lesson. Come 1653 and the apothecary Nicholas Culpeper published his famous *The English Physician, or Herball.* Note he calls it English. For the first time a writer dared to translate the Latin medical texts into the common language; it was through this Latin that the surgeons had been keeping control over their ministry in just the same way as the pre-Reformation Church had used Latin for its services. That an apothecary (less than a surgeon) should have such impudence caused outrage among the surgeons for now the common people had access to herbal knowledge for treating themselves. That was not good news for a surgeon's bank balance! Culpeper's oak remedies were exploiting the tree's astringent qualities and people still use them today. All Culpeper's entries start with astrology and so the old faiths come to the fore again, since he says oak is under the dominion of Jupiter, and we have met with that already. Jupiter of course was the Roman counterpart of the Greek Zeus and he too had the lightning oak as his sacred tree. Today, with all the advances in medicine we have not abandoned the oak. For example, it is used in homeopathy while in the Bach flower remedies oak is for strong, steady people who never give up under adversity, and doesn't that sound just like the Saxons and other pioneering peoples met with earlier in this quest !

LAST WORDS

The social history of the oak persists today. The Men of Kent, for example, carry holm-oak boughs on formal occasions. That is to commemorate them being granted a continuation of their Saxon rights and privileges by William the Conqueror. He had been surrounded by men of Kent camouflaged under oak boughs and when they showed themselves, fully armed, to demand their rights they left William worried that there might be a whole load more of them in the woods so he prudently granted their wishes. To celebrate this victory, the motto of Kent is 'Invictor' – unconquered, and they also placed a memorial beside the A2 in 1958, (later moved to Swanscombe churchyard). Thus to all true Kentish Men and Men of Kent the monarch is named as William I, William of Normandy or William the Bastard but never William the *Conqueror*!

Additions to the story are still being created. In Norwich Cathedral on 17 November 1996 there was a service of remembrance for the injured and bereaved through road accidents. Their names were inscribed on oak leaves and carried forward by their relatives to be placed at the foot of the Easter candle. Apparently the original plan was for children to give each member of the congregation an acorn but they could not find any and planned to collect oak leaves to light a perpetual flame on Easter Sunday instead.

Here ends the quest for the sacred oak but only because it has been brief. As you will have gathered on reading through to here, there are major topics that fill big text books in their own right, so there is plenty more to explore in relation to the mighty oak. Some of it is trapped in our English language, so there is the familiar proverb that *'From little acorns mighty oaks do grow.'* Another says, '*It takes many strokes to fell an oak,'* and our oaks are certainly not down yet. Even if the new threat from the 'Sudden Oak Death' disease causes mass casualties it will still be in the language. All my life I have heard country people refer to the 'trusty' oak but I've only just found out that in ancient languages the word for *tree* also meant *trust,* as in the Saxon word *treow.* Before the English were learning the Roman alphabet there was another way of writing, for the word 'write' meant originally 'to score with a sharp tool' and referred to cutting lines into a surface. We call them runes. They were in existence by the 2nd century and there was a specific rune for 'oak.' The peoples who wrote in runes have left us some very profound and beautiful 'poems.' This one embodies so much that we have met in this quest for the sacred oak.

Oak is for the sons of men on earth
A feeder of flesh often travels
Over gannet's bath, the ocean tests
Whether the oak keeps good faith.[58]

ACKNOWLEDGEMENT
Many thanks to Ruth Wylie, national authority on the Green Man, for reviewing that chapter and for granting the reproduction rights for the four photographs which are all hers.

NOTES AND SOURCES

[1] Pryor, Francis; 2001; *Seahenge*; Harper Collins

[2] For more information on Iceman there is a range of books in print at present.

[3] Generally listed as 'Iron Age' but St. George's began in the late Bronze Age and St. Anne's has never been excavated.

[4] For purposes of objectivity the Christian system of dating BC/AD has been updated to the more neutral BCE (Before Common Era) and CE (Common Era).

[5] de bello Gallico, 6.17.1

[6] There is a proposal that this blending of Lugus with Wodan/Odin might have occurred on the borders of the Celtic/Germanic world, possibly with the Chatti people, of Hesse, during the Late Iron Age.

[7] an inscribed lead plate found near Chalamiers in South West France has a Celtic text that presents considerable linguistic difficulties but part of it is thought to read, "*I prepare them for Lugus,*" meaning the slain enemies are offered to the god in return for victory.

[8] To put this in context see John King's *The Celtic Druid's Year: Seasonal Cycles of the Ancient Celts; Blanford; 1994*

[9] In this book, the Germanic word 'heathen' has been used for north west Europe but the Latin 'pagan' for Roman/Christian viewpoints.

[10] For details, examples and bibiliography see the excellent survey by Francis Pryor, *Britain AD*; HarperCollinsPublishers; 2004

[11] There are seven pages of useful maps in Kathleen Herbert, *Looking for the Lost Gods of England;* Anglo-Saxon Books; 1994

[12] The study of place-names reveals that those thought to derive from Tiw are all outside the Danelaw (with the exception of Tysoe in Warwickshire), suggesting this name was restricted to Saxon usage.

[13] From Janaway, John, 1983, *The Story of Godalming*; Local Heritage Books, Newbury; p.15

[14] See Malden, H. E. ed.; 1911; *The Victoria History of the County of Surrey*

[15] See 'Saxon Surrey' by Rob Poulton in Bird, Joanna and D.G.; *The Archaeology of Surrey to 1540;* Surrey Arch. Soc.; 1987

[16] MS Cod.pal., 577, Vatican Library

[17] Davidson, H. R. Ellis; 1964; *Gods and Myths of Northern Europe*; Penguin. p.60

[18] Quoted by Ellis Davidson, p.59

[19] There's archaeological evidence from the Bronze Age for this and it is unlikely that it would have been given up by this date. One of the herbs used for certain was Henbane. There are hints of alcohol use from Saxon Surrey.

[20] Probably not. There is archaeological evidence that Henbane was used in ancient rituals for its hallucinogenic properties but it is to be doubted whether they could get enough of the seed for all the assembly all the time. In any case, universal use would detract from the power of the shaman.

[21] Known also as The Chariot of Thor who was Odin's son.
[22] The last time success in conflict was attributed to Odin was when an inferior force of Swedes beat the Danes at the Battle on Lena in 1208.
[23] Author of the *History of the Archbishops of Hamburg-Bremen – Gesta Hammaburgensis ecclesiae pontificum.* He reported the sacrifices from an informant but did not see them himself.
[24] See *Ynglinga Saga*
[25] One exception was Snorri Sturluson (1179-1241), the Icelandic writer of the famous Prose Edda. At one point he says Thor *was* the son of Odin and in another place he reverses it
[26] *Flateyjarbók,* 1. 268. A manuscript of sagas about the Norwegian kings, written at Flatey monastery in Iceland. The temple was at Thrandheim.
[27] Quoted by Davidson from c. Marstrander. 'Thor en Irlande', *Revue Celtique,* 36, 1915-16. pp.241 ff.
[28] Davidson, p.77
[29] *Kjalnesinga Saga;* Icelandic
[30] There is a detailed description of a temple in section four of the *Eyrbyggja Saga;* Icelandic.
[31] At Thorsness, on the Broadfjörd.
[32] *Eyrbyggja Saga.* His arrival is recorded in the *Lándnamabók.*
[33] Venerable Bede, *A History of the English Church and People,* Ch.13
[34] This complicated concept is explored with full sources by William Chaney in *The Cult of Kingship in Anglo-Saxon England: the transition from paganism to Christianity.* Manchester University Press, 1970
[35] his queen, Bertha, was Christian already
[36] See the history of Fishbourne Roman Palace. It was to right of spire in illus.
[37] In contrast, at least two kings, Sigeberht of East Anglia (circa 630-7) and Caedwalla of Wessex (680s), abdicated to become penitents.
[38] St. John's Day is 24th June which is not now considered to coincide with the Midsummer's Day/shortest day but that is because the earth wobbles on its axis, moving the dates up and down the calendar. The same applies to the conversion of the pagan Roman Saturnalia that became Christmas so the date of Christmas varies also, e.g. 6th January in the Armenian Church.
[39] Oak was not accepted universally as the timber of the Cross; other trees were included in this part of the Faith.
[40] This spoils the tradition that the body of St Edmund rested in this church over night on its way to its burial place in the monastery at Bury St Edmunds since that was in 1013. It must have been an earlier building. The present one is nevertheless the oldest timber building in Britain.
[41] The two types may well originate from different sources, to be united during medieval times and have remained in partnership since. Those with foliage emanating from the mouth and head are known rather ingloriously as

'disgorging' heads and these can be found in Indian temples. There is current speculation that the image travelled the Silk Road to China and came back again. The mask type appears on Roman monuments.

[42] She assumed that the image was synonymous with Jack-in-the-Green, which can be refuted on evidential grounds, along with Robin Hood connections etc. but her idea has caused confusion ever since.

[43] The image persisted after the Reformation, primarily as a secular image, and can be followed right through to the present time when you can buy one cast in concrete from many a garden centre. For an excellent study that includes the post-Reformation periods see Mercia MacDermott, *Explore Green Men;* Heart of Albion Press; 2006

[44] The number is increased by their use in decorative schemes upon tombs placed therein, telling us about the piety of the deceased rather than the decoration of the church fabric.

[45] The image starts to occur in illuminated manuscripts at the end of the 10th century and later in carved stone (Mercia MacDermott p.138)

[46] For the few Continental examples at this period see MacDermott.

[47] According to Ronald Hutton, *The Stations of the Sun;* 1996. (p.226 paperback ed. 1997)

[48] *Councils and Synods…1205-1313,* eds. F. M. Powicke and C. R. Cheney; Oxford, 1964. 480

[49] It is popularly believed that some of the 'foliage' folk customs still enacted around the country devolved from this but research has proven that the medieval folk customs were suppressed at the Reformation and it was not until the 19th century that the chimney sweeps created a new one. The modern Green Man festivities, such as those at Hastings and Rochester are modern inventions. See for example Roy Judge (1979) *The Jack in the Green;* Folklore Soc. and Keith Leech, *The Hastings Jack in the Green.*

[50] Photo on p.84 of MacDermott.

[51] Normally it is three lobes per leaf but beware of presuming this connects with the Holy Trinity and must be Christian. The number 3 was sacred in religions long before Christianity. Apart from that, it is a balanced design and the craftsmen, even of 'crude' work, loved designs that pleased the eye.

[52] Details from the archives of Chertsey Museum.

[53] *Fragmenta H. Omont No.3*

[54] From Pollington, Stephen (2000); *Leechcraft: Early English Charms, Plant Lore, and Healing.* Anglo-Saxon Books. p.76.

[55] It is Recipe 8 of part III; for original and translation see Pollington pp. 384-5. The recipe requires 43 different herbs.

[56] Pollington p.436

[57] Pollington p.494

[58] Translation from Pollington p.505

INDEX